I0824285

NOTRE-DAME

LYNN CURLEE

NOTRE-DAME

The World's Cathedral

Atheneum Books for Young Readers
NEW YORK · AMSTERDAM/ANTWERP · LONDON
TORONTO · SYDNEY/MELBOURNE · NEW DELHI

PROLOGUE

THE POINT ZERO OF FRANCE

There are a few monumental structures on Earth that can be considered among the most remarkable achievements of humanity. Besides their importance as architecture, they have come to represent the highest aspirations of people throughout the ages. A short list of some of these marvels must include: the Great Pyramid of Giza, the Parthenon in Athens, the Roman Pantheon, the Taj Mahal in India, the Great Wall of China, Angkor Wat in Cambodia, and the Cathedral of Notre-Dame in Paris.

As the capital of France and the unofficial cultural capital of Western Europe, Paris is a city of famous monuments. The Eiffel Tower, the Arc de Triomphe, and the Louvre Museum, once the vast royal palace of French kings, are renowned throughout the world. But the most famous, the most ancient, and certainly the most important Parisian monument is the Cathedral of Notre-Dame. It dominates the very center of Paris from its site on the Île de la Cité (City Island), a small island in the middle of the River Seine, which flows through the heart of the metropolis.

A **cathedral** is the home church of a bishop—an important official in the governing hierarchy of Catholicism. Notre-Dame is a Gothic cathedral, which means it was constructed in a very specific style in fashion for a few centuries during the Middle Ages. It stands on a parapet high above the Seine, and from across the river, the immense cathedral—with its complex, dynamic structure; massive towers; and lofty spire—recalls a magnificent "galleon under full sail." As you enter the cavernous interior through elaborately carved **portals**, your eyes gradually adjust to the relatively subdued light—sunlight filtered and transformed by enormous stained-glass windows that glow with a jewellike radiance. The rhythmic repetition of architectural details draws your gaze to the altar, far away at the other end of the church, and upward to the soaring vaulted stone ceiling high above. Completely removed from the bustling city outside,

The western front façade of the Cathedral of Notre-Dame, which serves as the main entrance for visitors

the atmosphere inside is resonant with history and the majestic, mystical, and awe-inspiring.

Notre-Dame has stood for nearly nine centuries as the symbolic spiritual and geographic heart of France. Directly in front of the portals, a small stone-and-brass plaque is set into the pavement of the **parvis**, the cathedral plaza. It marks the Point Zero of France, from which all distances in the country are measured. The visionary builders of Notre-Dame began with the tradition of building monumental structures of stone, inherited from the ancient world. By combining certain brilliant technical innovations with traditional forms and methods, they pushed a new style of architecture made of stone and glass to the very limit of what was possible.

In French, *Notre Dame* means "Our Lady"—the cathedral is dedicated to the Virgin Mary, mother of Christ. Over the centuries, the grand edifice has endured the reigns of thirty-three kings, three emperors, and five republics. It has been scarred by a bloody revolution and several wars. It has been neglected and repaired, renovated and restored. It has been celebrated as the subject of paintings, books, and movies, and it has become one of the world's great tourist attractions, drawing an average of twelve million visitors each year. They come to be astonished by the grandeur of its architecture and inspired by the otherworldly atmosphere of the world's most famous cathedral.

I was twenty-two years old in 1970 when I first visited Paris as a backpacking art history graduate student. In high school I had written an essay about the Cathedral of Notre-Dame, and in college we studied medieval architecture in depth. So I was particularly eager to see Notre-Dame in person. Seven years before, decades of urban grime had been scrubbed from the pale tan limestone in celebration of the cathedral's eight hundredth anniversary. For me it was an incredible experience. It was everything I had imagined.

In 2019 the entire world reacted in shock as the Cathedral of Notre-Dame came within a hairbreadth of being completely destroyed by fire while we all watched in real time on TV and online. The spontaneous outpouring of emotion and heartfelt concern from around the globe sealed Notre-Dame's unofficial status as "the World's Cathedral" once and for all. In a terrible instant, we almost lost it forever . . . but then we didn't.

Notre-Dame interior

PART I

THE CATHEDRAL IS BURNING!

On Monday of Holy Week, April 15, 2019, six days before Easter, a priest was celebrating the last Mass of the day in front of hundreds of worshippers in the hushed atmosphere of the Cathedral of Notre-Dame. It was precisely 6:18 p.m. when a red warning light suddenly flashed on the master smoke-alarm panel in the church's security office. The employee monitoring the panel was new on the job—he had been hired only three days before—and he had been at work since 7:00 a.m. His replacement hadn't shown up, so he was working a second shift.

The alarm indicated the location of the smoke, and he immediately radioed a church guard stationed in the cathedral to go check "the attic" for fire. As the worshippers and tourists were evacuated, the guard went to inspect the attic of the sacristy, a separate building in the cathedral complex. He found no fire there . . . because he had gone to the wrong attic.

This simple miscommunication was very nearly a fatal error. There was indeed a fire, but it was in the attic above the stone **vaults** that form the actual ceiling of the cathedral itself. *This* attic is a complex construction of wooden **trusses** called "the Forest." It supports the high, steeply pitched roof, covered in lead panels, that protects the stone vaults from weather. The massive oak timbers of the Forest were part of the original structure of the cathedral, more than eight hundred years old, dry, and extremely flammable. At 6:43 p.m. there was a second alarm signal. This time the guard went to the correct attic. He climbed three hundred narrow spiraling stone steps to discover part of the Forest in flames and the enclosed attic space filled with smoke. There were no fire walls or sprinklers, and despite the high-tech alarm system, human error had allowed the fire to spread out of control before it was discovered.

Finally, at 6:48 p.m., a half hour after the first

A "gargoyle" sculpture from the gallery of chimeras

alarm, the fire department was called. People on the street saw smoke beginning to pour from the upper parts of the cathedral. At 6:52 p.m. someone posted on Twitter, "I think Notre-Dame is burning." Within minutes, the word spread around the globe that the world's most famous cathedral was on fire. Crowds of shocked and horrified people began to gather along the riverbanks and bridges that spanned the Seine.

By the time the first team of firefighters arrived just before 7:00 p.m., thick smoke was obscuring the cathedral towers, and flames were visible. Corporal Miriam Chudzinski was a member of that first team. As they approached the scene, the sheer immensity of the cathedral obscured the view of the fire from their truck. "It might have been better like that," she recalled, since they didn't yet know the seriousness of what they would be confronting. Their job was to head directly to the burning attic to find out. She and her crew climbed the dark and narrow staircase, each bearing fifty-five pounds of gear and breathing apparatus. They knew their way, having done practice drills in the cathedral before, when "it was so peaceful, so quiet. . . . But that night, it was more like hell," with the Forest ablaze. The firefighters attached their hoses to the water risers and began working to try to contain the fire, which was spreading rapidly.

In the meantime, other fire crews had arrived and were battling the flames from the ground and from cherry pickers with dousing guns, which pumped water from the river. Eventually, there were nearly five hundred firefighters working in and around various parts of the cathedral. By now the interior of the attic was an inferno. The fire had spread to the famous flèche, the massive spire of heavy oak and lead that rises to a height of 315 feet from the very center of the building. The firefighters inside could not see it, but to the thousands of spectators who were watching from the streets and an audience of millions who were now livestreaming the event, the burning spire resembled an immense blazing torch, with the roof in flames all around.

At about 7:50 p.m., an hour into the firefight, the spectators on the ground and the entire world reacted in stunned disbelief as the spire teetered, then collapsed, and 750 tons of flaming debris came crashing down. Corporal Chudzinski described a deafening blast like "a giant bulldozer dropping dozens of stones into a dumpster."

All the cathedral doors were slammed shut by the pressure from the blast, and a fireball hurtled

A cathedral guard discovering the attic ablaze and full of smoke

through the attic. The firefighters would have been incinerated if they had not happened to be behind a barrier at that moment. Several stone vaults at the center of the cathedral gave way under the impact, and tons of broken stone, burning timbers, flaming sparks, and a shower of molten lead rained down into the interior of the cathedral itself. Corporal Chudzinski recalled, "I felt useless, ridiculously small. . . . I was just powerless."

Now the flames, fanned by a brisk wind, were threatening the north tower of the façade. Inside the two towers are the **belfries**, huge frameworks of massive oak beams that support the famed bronze bells of Notre-Dame. The north tower houses eight of these enormous bells, which weigh many tons each. If the wooden belfry of the north tower burned and collapsed, the heavy bells would become virtual "wrecking balls" and could bring down the tower. In that case, a chain reaction would likely cause the south tower to collapse as well, and the entire edifice of the cathedral would almost certainly come crashing down.

At about 8:30 p.m. French President Emmanuel Macron and other government officials arrived on the scene for a briefing by General Jean-Claude Gallet, head of the Paris Fire Brigade. He gave them the appallingly bad news. By now it was clear that the roof was almost completely destroyed, so while the men on the ground continued to douse what remained, General Gallet gave the order for the frontline firefighters to cut their losses and concentrate on saving the north tower. "In twenty minutes, I'll know if we've lost it," he predicted. President Macron's stunned silence signaled his approval, and the second phase of the battle to save Notre-Dame began.

According to the *New York Times*, police drone footage from high above revealed to the world the cathedral's roof as "a fiery cross illuminating the night sky. At the center was a gaping black hole where the spire had stood." The massive timbers of the north tower belfry were now beginning to catch fire, so the decision was made to approach the flames by taking additional hoses up the south tower. It was a high-risk strategy that would expose the firefighters to mortal danger without a sure escape route. As thick smoke billowed from the north tower, Master Sergeant Rémi Lemaire led a crew of volunteers up the steps of the south tower, and they set up a command platform between the towers. From there they dropped their hoses over the side to connect with fire trucks on the ground and then entered the burning north tower. As they climbed the narrow steps, some of the firefighters

The spire of Notre-Dame toppling over

were dousing the floor beneath them while others were working to soak the flaming belfry. They were fully aware that if the belfry collapsed, they would likely all be killed, and the cathedral would be demolished. Gradually, they worked their way up higher and higher, past the sets of enormous bells, and finally, by about 9:45 p.m., their heroic effort succeeded in taming the flames. The fight was not over—the cathedral was smoldering, and there were small fires here and there to be quenched—but the real crisis was past. Miraculously, there were no serious injuries, and no lives had been lost.

At 11:00 p.m. General Gallet told President Macron he was confident that the fires in the tower were under control, but the Cathedral of Notre-Dame was seriously damaged—perhaps fatally. The roof was gone. The central ceiling vaults had collapsed. The interior was filled with charred debris. Pulverized toxic lead had contaminated the surrounding area. No one knew whether the basic structure was still sound. Could it all be salvaged and repaired, or would it have to be demolished?

At 11:30 p.m. the president of France addressed his nation and the world on TV from the parvis in front of the cathedral. "The worst was avoided, even though the battle is not yet over," he declared. Then he made a solemn pledge: "We will rebuild this cathedral together."

Parisian firefighters in the north tower belfry

PART 2

"A . . . SYMPHONY IN STONE"—VICTOR HUGO

The island now called the Île de la Cité was originally settled around 250 BC by the Parisii, "the boat people," a Celtic tribe. Today the city of Paris bears their name. When the Romans invaded the region, which they called Gaul, in 52 BC, they captured and occupied the island. It became an important outpost of the Roman Empire and a hub for local trade and commerce. The Romans built a small temple to Jupiter on the eastern end of the island. After Christianity became the official Roman religion in the year AD 313, over time a complex of religious buildings arose on the former site of the pagan temple. The largest of these was a cathedral that was probably dedicated to Saint Stephen, traditionally regarded as the first Christian martyr, who was stoned to death for his beliefs.

In ancient Rome a **basilica** was a large roofed public meeting hall. Basilicas were usually rectangular and divided lengthwise into **aisles**. A wide, tall central area called a **nave** was flanked on each side by one or two narrower aisles with lower ceilings, all separated by rows of columns. Many early Christian churches adopted the layout of Roman basilicas. Saint Stephen's was one of these, but since the Cathedral of Notre-Dame would later be built overlapping the same site, reusing many of the same stones, few traces of the first cathedral remain.

The Roman Empire collapsed by AD 476, but by then Latin culture and the Catholic Church were established in Gaul. Gradually, over a few centuries, the kingdom of the Franks came to dominate the region, and so Gaul became France, with Paris as its capital. The turn of the millennium, in the year 1000, came and went without the world ending in catastrophe, which had been predicted and widely feared. A collective wave of relief spread all over Christendom, and a great era of church building began. In northern Europe, basilica-plan churches were built in the Romanesque style, a straightforward construction with thick masonry walls, often supporting enormously heavy stone ceilings

A heron sculpture from the gallery of chimeras

called vaults. Windows were necessarily very small, since large ones would seriously weaken the load-bearing walls. Romanesque churches were somber—dark and enclosed, with the atmosphere of a mysterious "fortress of God" keeping the forces of evil at bay in a hostile world. These buildings were impressive but had certain limitations. Churches capped by thick, heavy stone vaults could only be so wide and so tall, and windows could only be so big without compromising the stability of the structure.

In the first decades of the twelfth century, Catholic theologians in Paris proposed a new vision. Instead of a fortress of God, a cathedral should be a model of Heaven, filled with the "light of Divine Essence, that illuminates the darkness, reveals truth, and is the source of all creation, filtering through radiant stained-glass windows and bathing the interior with a glow not quite of this world. To allow more of this magic light to enter, architects were to pare their structures to the bone, defying the laws of gravity in ever higher and more delicate buildings" (Swaan, p. 48). They did it by taking the vaulted Romanesque basilica plan and combining it with certain technical advances.

These innovations—pointed arches, ribbed vaults, and **flying buttresses**—defined the new Gothic style of architecture. They made it possible for the structure of a church to be a skeleton of stone with translucent walls of stained glass instead of thick, massive walls of masonry. These features had all been used before individually, but they were first combined in renovating part of a Romanesque church, the Abbey of Saint-Denis, near Paris. This renovation is considered to be the first Gothic structure. A few years later, the Gothic innovations were combined in a single unified design for a new building to replace the old basilica of Saint Stephen in Paris. The new church would be dedicated to "Our Lady." It would be the first completely Gothic cathedral, planned from the ground up to express the new theology of light. The Cathedral of Notre-Dame would be built at a truly colossal scale with vaults far higher and windows far bigger than had ever been attempted before.

For the people who built it, the Gothic Cathedral of Notre-Dame was many things: a model of the celestial city of Heaven, God's home on Earth, a ship for believers navigating their spiritual journey through the world, a sanctuary from the storms of life, a treasury for precious holy objects, and a picture book of religious images. It was the center of the community, a demonstration of prosperity, and an object of civic pride, towering over the medieval city.

GOTHIC VAULT

BARREL VAULT RIBBED VAULT

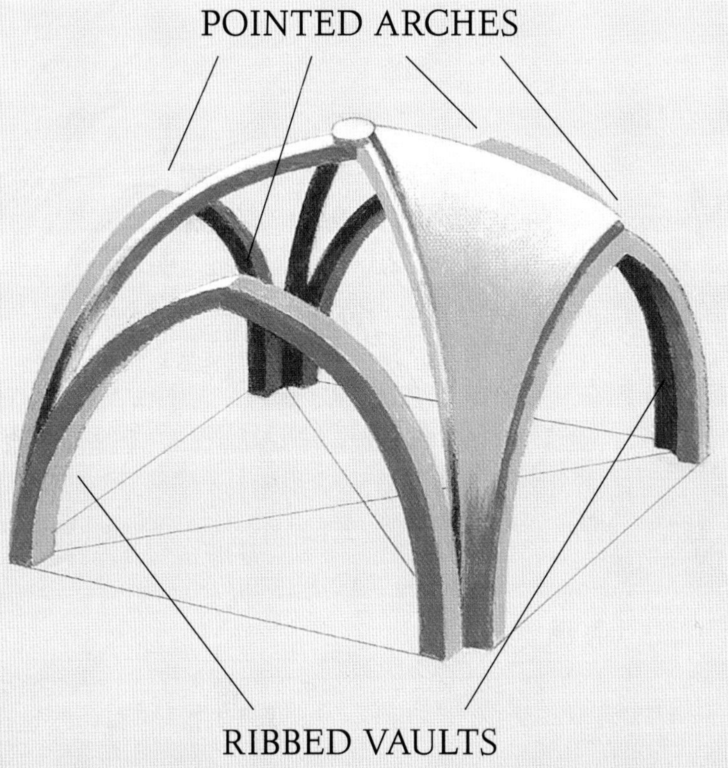

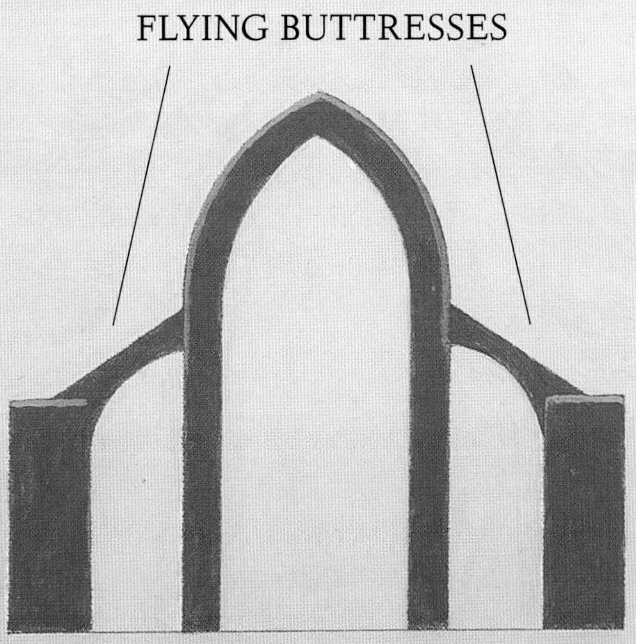

THE TECHNICAL INNOVATIONS OF GOTHIC ARCHITECTURE

- Pointed arches are stronger and distribute weight differently compared to round arches. They appear to soar upward and are the signature form of Gothic architecture.
- Reinforcing vaulted ceilings with stone **ribs** allows a vault to be a thin, much lighter membrane of stone, like the taut fabric canopy of an umbrella supported by metal spokes. The ribs carry the weight instead of thick load-bearing walls.
- Arched supports called flying buttresses transfer the weight of the vaults to massive **piers** placed at strategic points around the outside of the building, like several people propping up a heavy cupboard with outstretched arms.

Medieval cathedrals were planned and constructed without working drawings or blueprints. The architects conceived a grand overall design and conveyed what they wanted with verbal instructions and simple sketches on parchment or temporary plaster panels. The technical Gothic innovations were first developed by trial and error. The only way to determine whether a ribbed vault or flying buttress would work was to build it and see if it stood or collapsed. A cathedral was first laid out on the ground according to what were considered sacred and universal harmonious geometric principles with measuring rods, stakes, and rope. Besides determining the design, architects also directed the construction. They were hands-on master craftsmen who were trained as both stonemasons and woodworkers, since very precise wooden forms had to be crafted to support stone arches and vaults as they were being built.

Gothic cathedrals are among the most complex and ambitious structures ever conceived. It is simply mind-boggling to realize that they were constructed completely by manual labor, without the aid of machines of any kind. There were obviously no computers for design work, mathematical calculations, or virtual modeling, and no electric, hydraulic, or steam-powered devices to make things easier. All they had were hand tools like chisels, mallets, handsaws, levers, winches, and pulleys. Building materials were transported by boat or by oxcart. Probably the most complicated device they used was like a big hamster wheel, large enough for several men to operate by walking inside, for hoisting heavy loads high into the air.

The massive workforce included quarrymen, carters for transporting supplies, stone carvers and stonemasons, carpenters, blacksmiths, skilled

Nave of Notre-Dame

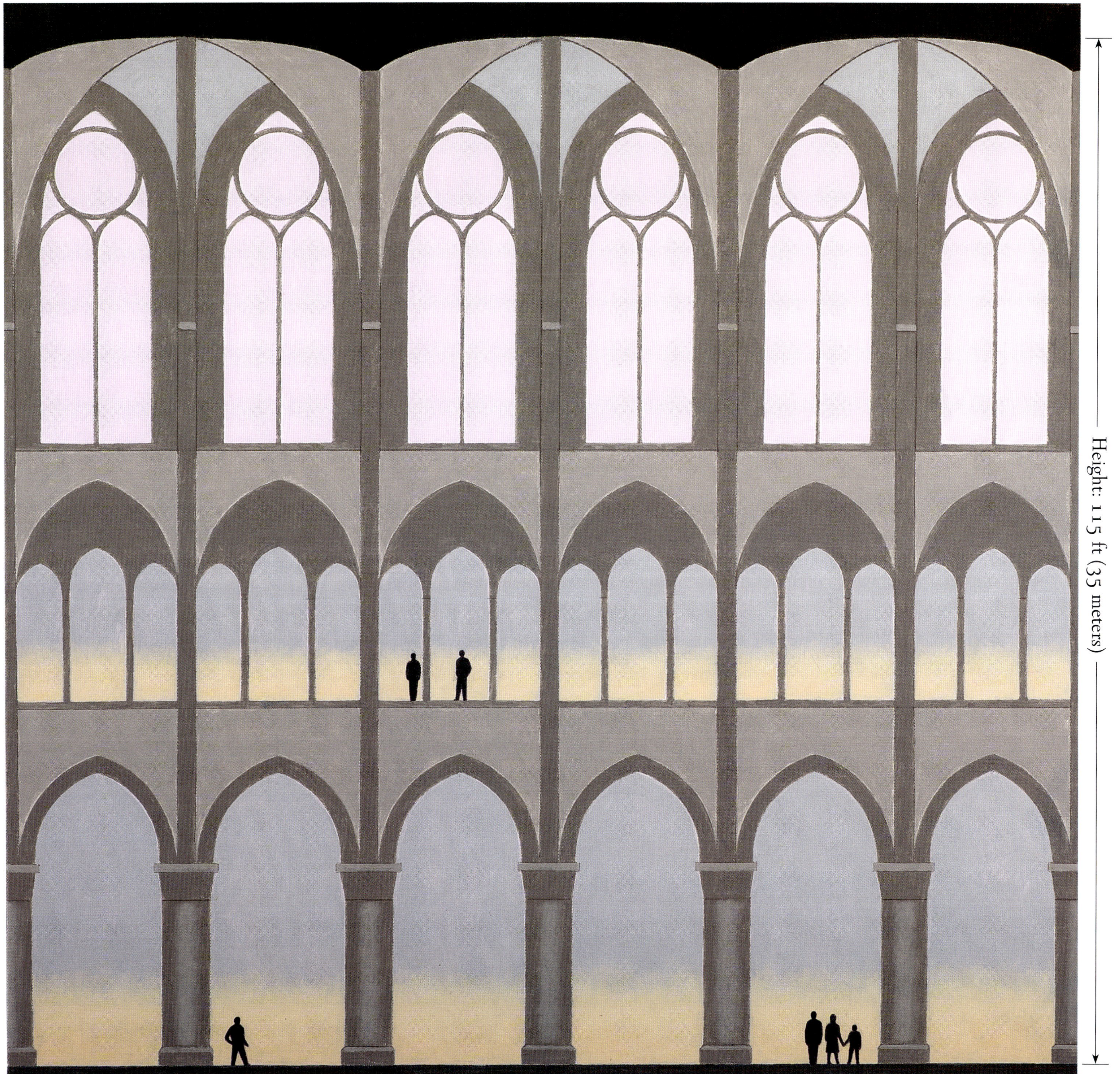
Height: 115 ft (35 meters)

NOTRE-DAME FLOOR PLAN

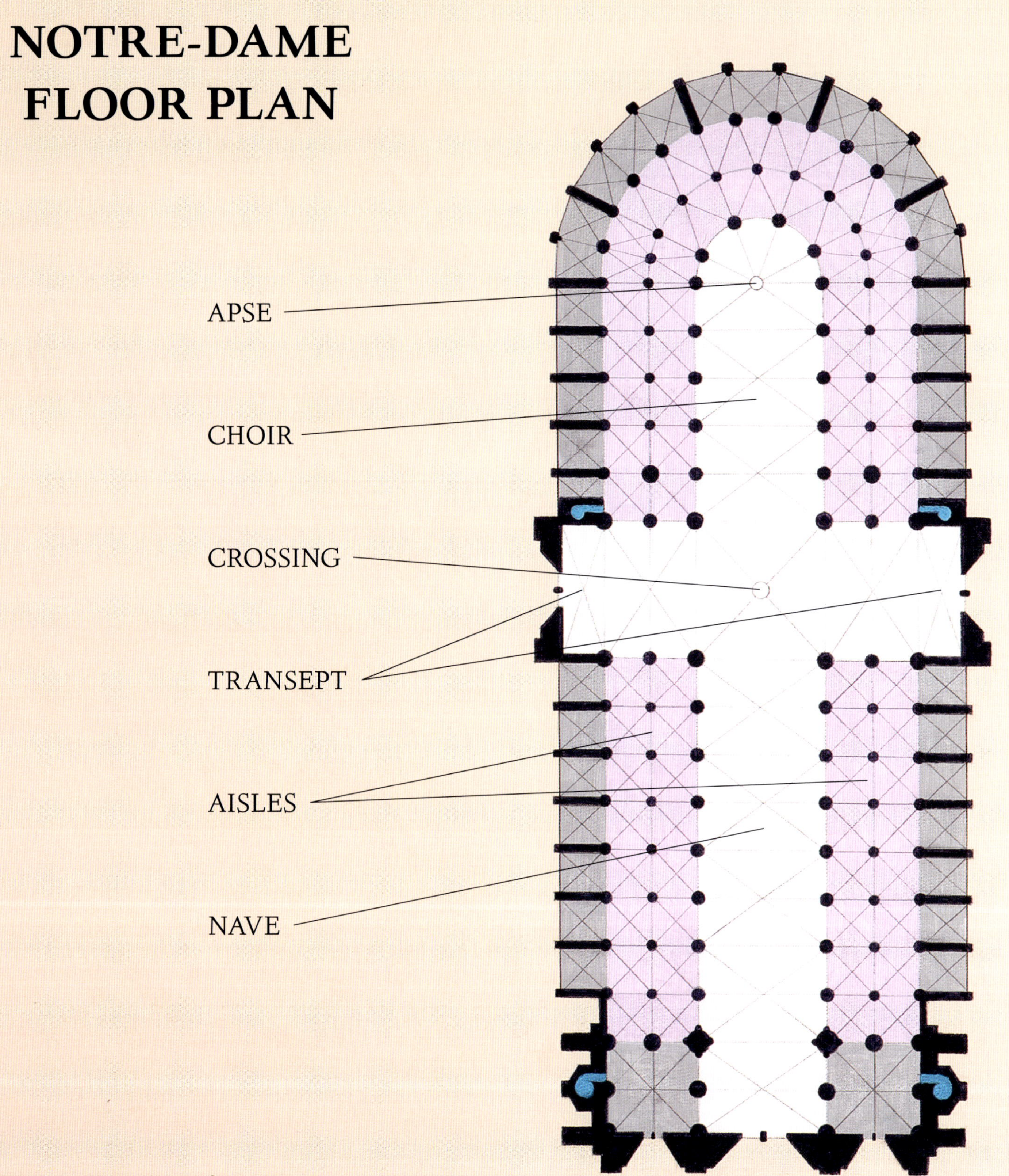

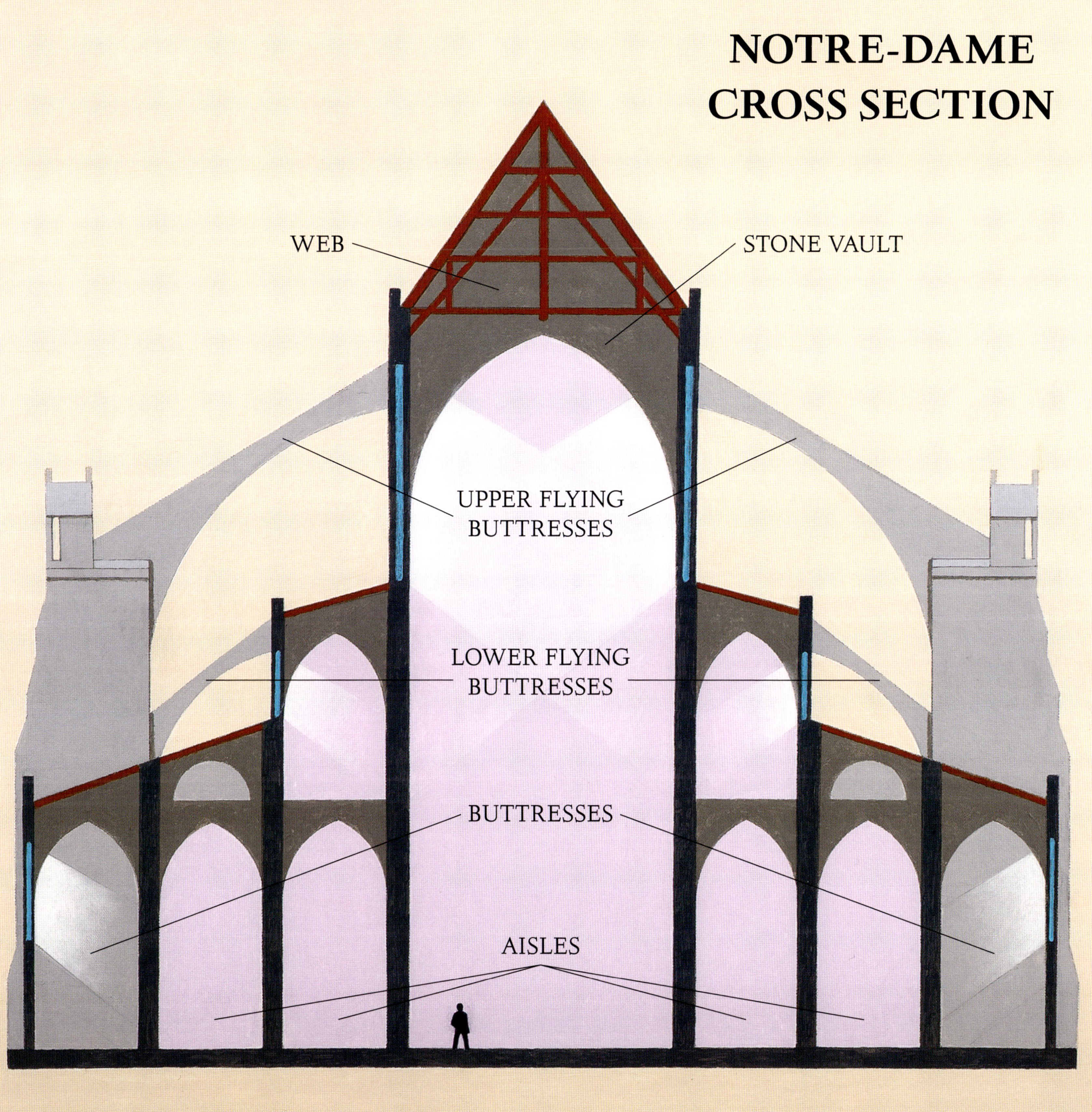
NOTRE-DAME
CROSS SECTION
WEB
STONE VAULT
UPPER FLYING
BUTTRESSES
LOWER FLYING
BUTTRESSES
BUTTRESSES
AISLES

sculptors, glaziers for manufacturing and installing stained glass, painters and plasterers, plus all the supporting workers who provided the unskilled labor. In an era when the concept of Heaven and Hell were very real, the entire population of a town contributed in some way to the construction of their cathedral for the prestige of their community and to the greater glory of God.

Construction on Notre-Dame began in 1163 at the eastern end and proceeded rapidly but intermittently in several different phases. The **choir** with its altar was built first and in use by the mid-1180s. In 1200 the nave and the west front were nearing completion, and by 1250 the massive towers were finished. Even though the cathedral as originally planned was complete, for the next century, until the mid-1300s, changes and additions kept new generations of architects and craftsmen busy.

Chapels were added between the exterior buttressing piers. The **clerestory** windows directly under the high vaults were enlarged, flying buttresses were modified, and the **transept** was extended to include two gigantic and elaborate new **rose windows**.

During the Middle Ages, the vast majority of people were illiterate. Notre-Dame was planned as a kind of biblical picture book with illustrations of sculpture and stained glass. The sculptures were concentrated in the three great portals of the western façade. The two side portals were dedicated to the life of the Virgin Mary, while the most important central portal depicted Christ on a throne presiding over the Last Judgment of souls, with an apocalyptic vision of Heaven and Hell. Above the portals, a gallery of twenty-eight kings of Judah runs the entire width of the façade. These imposing figures are nearly twelve feet tall. Besides the important façade sculptures, the cathedral fairly bristles with carved architectural details—**turrets**, **finials**, **crockets**, **balustrades**, and **gargoyle** rainspouts. Most of the sculptures and carved details were originally painted or gilded in an exuberant display of color that matched the jewellike richness of the medieval stained glass, the magical quality of which has never been surpassed or even equaled, since the exact process of making it was a closely guarded secret.

By the time the construction was completely finished, Gothic churches had been built all over Europe. But Notre-Dame was one of the very first, and as the Cathedral of Paris, then the largest city in northern Europe, Notre-Dame—with the grandeur of its massive towers and its dazzling array of soaring flying buttresses radiating from the **apse** like a fairy-tale vision—has always been the most important and iconic of them all.

The central portal of the western façade featuring a gallery of kings

PART 3
NINE CENTURIES OF HISTORY

From the beginning, the Cathedral of Notre-Dame was closely associated with the monarchy of France. King Louis VII supported the project of replacing the old Cathedral of Saint Stephen with both enthusiasm and money. When the cornerstone of the new church was laid in 1163, the king was in attendance at the ceremony led by Pope Alexander III. As the location for both the king's residence and the country's most important Catholic church, the Île de la Cité was the center of power in France.

After the mid-1300s, when the cathedral had been completed, Notre-Dame remained basically unchanged for the next two centuries. But the 1500s were a period of unrest. French protestants, called Huguenots, faced intense persecution and rebelled against what they considered the "false" religion of Catholicism with its rituals, religious images, wealth, and power. The rebellion turned violent. "Churches were sacked, images smashed and burned, relics destroyed, and sanctuaries desecrated" (Felix, p. 46). We have few details, but in 1548 Notre-Dame itself was raided and pillaged. The French Wars of Religion raged on until the end of the century.

In the late 1600s and early 1700s, during the long reign of King Louis XIV, Notre-Dame was altered because it was now considered old-fashioned and out of style. The interior was redecorated in the Baroque manner of the era. Many of the original carved wooden medieval furnishings were replaced with new ones. An elaborate ironwork grill was installed to separate the choir from the nave. A gleaming, new, sculpted marble altarpiece was installed with a Pietà—the Virgin Mary holding the dead body of Christ—in the center, flanked by the figures of Louis XIII and Louis XIV kneeling in adoration. The central portal of the west front was modified to allow royal carriages to enter in processions. Much of

A monstrous "gargoyle" sculpture from the gallery of chimeras

the glorious medieval stained glass was replaced by panes of clear glass. Apparently, the "Sun King," Louis XIV, wanted actual sunlight in the cathedral. Thankfully, the two magnificent rose windows in the transepts and the smaller one in the western façade were spared.

During the French Revolution in the late 1700s, society was upended. Besides overthrowing the monarchy, a goal of the revolution was to replace Catholicism with a secular religion called Deism, a belief that divinity is revealed through nature rather than through official religious dogma. Churches were closed and ransacked. Notre-Dame was stripped of many of its furnishings, and the medieval portal sculptures were scarred and defaced. In 1793 a mob of revolutionaries destroyed all twenty-eight statues in the gallery of the kings of Judah, pulling them down with ropes tied around their necks to smash on the pavement of the parvis. Most of the cathedral bells were removed and melted down to make cannons.

In November of that same year, a pageant was held in the gutted cathedral, renamed the Temple of Reason. An elaborate stage set was constructed, and an actress was crowned Goddess of Reason, while other young women danced and sang hymns to liberty for an audience of revolutionary leaders. In the late 1790s, Notre-Dame was nearly utterly destroyed. There was a scheme to dismantle the cathedral and sell the stones and the metal roof for scrap.

The revolution, with its ideals of "Liberty, Equality, and Brotherhood," had become the bloody Reign of Terror, and the great masterpiece of Gothic architecture was now being used merely as an immense storage shed for munitions and wine.

The French Revolution finally ended when Napoleon Bonaparte, an ambitious general of the French army, staged a coup d'état in 1799. He was named consul of the new French Republic. As part of his strategic rise to power, he returned ownership of Notre-Dame to the Catholic Church. Four years later, Napoleon declared himself emperor of France. In an opulent display of vanity, his elaborate coronation ceremony was held in the Cathedral of Notre-Dame on Sunday, December 2, 1804. The battered old church was lavishly decorated with enormous tapestries and carpets and festooned with Napoleonic regalia. After being anointed by Pope Pius VII, Napoleon Bonaparte, draped in robes of red velvet and ermine, actually crowned *himself* emperor before crowning his wife Josephine as empress.

Eventually, Napoleon was deposed and sent into

Emperor Napoleon I

exile. In 1830 France became a constitutional monarchy. By now the Cathedral of Notre-Dame was in a sorry state of disrepair. Most of the damage done during the revolution had never been addressed—the interior was mostly stripped bare, the western façade with its array of medieval sculptures was badly battered, the original medieval spire had been torn down, and the exterior limestone was eroded, pitted, and stained with centuries of weather and grime. The great cathedral was dilapidated and on the verge of being considered an eyesore.

Victor Hugo was a French author renowned as a poet, novelist, essayist, and playwright during a long career. In 1831, when he was twenty-nine years old, Hugo published a novel that became a bestselling blockbuster—a book that made him famous and wealthy. Set in the fifteenth century, *The Hunchback of Notre Dame* is the tragic story of Quasimodo, a deformed, hideously ugly young man who had been orphaned as an infant and raised to be Notre-Dame's bell ringer after being taken in by Claude Frollo, archdeacon of the cathedral. Shunned as monstrous and deafened by daily close-up exposure to the pealing bells, Quasimodo has spent his entire sad life hiding in the nooks and corners of the immense cathedral to avoid being brutally mocked and taunted. He is befriended by Esmeralda, a beautiful young Gypsy, and falls hopelessly in love with her, but she is enthralled with Phoebus, a dashing cavalier. Frollo, the archdeacon, is revealed to be an evil man who can't be trusted. With a convoluted plot involving treachery and mistaken identity, today *The Hunchback of Notre Dame* reads as a grim melodrama, but it spotlights the cathedral itself as a major character in the story. Victor Hugo regarded the Cathedral of Notre-Dame as representing the pinnacle of French civilization. His immensely popular book drew attention to the artistic and historical importance of the "symphony in stone," while at the same time an emerging awareness of the cultural heritage of France was contributing to a new sense of national identity. As a result, an official committee was established to explore the idea of repairing and restoring Notre-Dame.

In 1844, after winning a competition for the job, two young architects, Eugène Viollet-le-Duc and Jean-Baptiste Lassus, were awarded the contract for the project. Work began with rebuilding some flying buttresses that were in danger of collapsing and continued with the restoration of the western façade. New statues and sculpted panels in the original medieval style were made to replace those that had been defaced or destroyed. Very little of

Quasimodo, the bell ringer

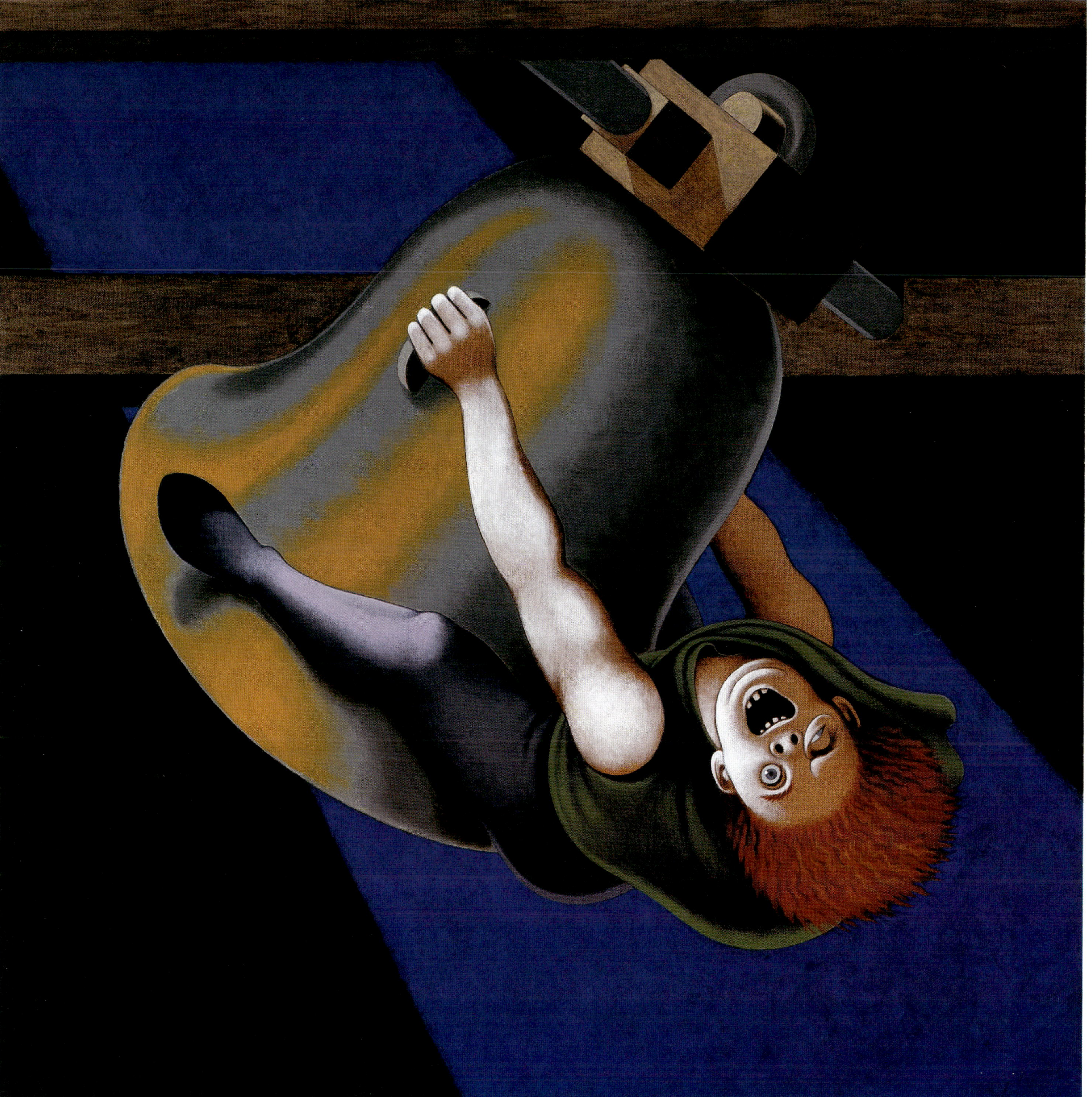

the original medieval stained glass remained, so many new windows were commissioned, and the effect of "translucent walls" was restored.

As the work progressed, besides repairing the damage and reproducing things that had been destroyed, the two architects began reworking parts of the building and adding new features. The flying buttresses of the choir were completely rebuilt and embellished with turrets and pinnacles. The south transept rose window was modified. Viollet-le-Duc designed a magnificent new spire in the authentic thirteenth-century style of the lost original, but on a grand new scale—topping off at 315 feet above the pavement, it reached as high as a thirty-story building.

One of the most famous and beloved features of Notre-Dame is the gallery of **chimeras**, an array of fifty-four sculpted creatures—demons, monsters, animals, and birds—that sit perched on a balustrade high up at the base of the bell towers. The statues look out upon the city of Paris as though guarding the cathedral. Some are whimsical, some frightening, others naturalistic. People are surprised to learn that they are not medieval at all but are completely the invention of Viollet-le-Duc. He designed them in the medieval style, and they were carved by a gifted sculptor named Victor Pyanet.

This approach was extremely controversial; many notable Frenchmen were opposed to the unhistorical additions. But when Lassus died in 1857, Viollet-le-Duc took complete charge and, dismissing his critics, single-mindedly pursued his personal vision of the *ideal* Gothic cathedral. His extensive reworking of Notre-Dame is now part of its history. The cathedral that we know today must be understood and appreciated as a creation of both the Middle Ages and the nineteenth century.

In the twentieth century, the Cathedral of Notre-Dame, and the city of Paris itself, survived two World Wars in which France was a primary target for German aggression. During World War I, German bombers attacked Paris several times; Notre-Dame received one direct hit, but the lead roof only sustained some minor damage. Early in World War II, the Nazi army captured Paris and occupied the French capital for four years until the city was liberated by Allied forces. As French and American soldiers were advancing toward the city, German führer Adolf Hitler issued an order to reduce Paris to a pile of rubble. But the German commander in charge of the city surrendered on August 25, 1944, before the order could be carried out. The next day, the liberation of Paris was celebrated with a parade from the Arc de Triomphe to

Workers restoring the rose window of the western façade

the Cathedral of Notre-Dame, where a Mass was held to commemorate the great event.

On a much lighter note, on the morning of June 26, 1971, twenty-one-year-old French aerialist Philippe Petit made news worldwide by performing his daredevil high-wire act while balancing on a cable he had somehow managed to string between the two bell towers of Notre-Dame, 225 feet above the parvis. The stunt was carefully planned; he had hidden in the cathedral overnight. The authorities were not amused, but the crowds of Parisians who gathered to watch were astonished and delighted.

Notre-Dame requires continual maintenance, and yet another restoration project was begun in 1991. Twentieth-century pollution from industry and car exhausts had eaten away at the porous limestone, and much of the exterior and its delicate ornamentation was replaced block by block in an extensive campaign lasting a decade. Then, in 2018, after 150 years, Viollet-le-Duc's spire of oak timbers encased in lead was in need of major repairs, so the central part of the cathedral was covered in metal scaffolding. It is likely that in the early evening of Monday, April 15, 2019, an electrical short circuit in the construction equipment sparked the disastrous blaze in the attic above the high vaults.

Philippe Petit performing his daredevil stunt

PART 4
AFTER THE FIRE, THE RESTORATION

After the catastrophe, stunned authorities struggled to determine exactly what had happened. Engineers were brought in to evaluate the structure, using lasers to scan for damage. The entire roof of Notre-Dame was completely destroyed, leaving the tops of the vaults covered with charred timbers and exposed to the weather. The impact of the collapsing spire had caused the central vaults to give way, making an enormous, gaping, jagged hole with the interior of the cathedral open to the sky. The interior was littered with approximately eight hundred tons of debris contaminated by molten lead and toxic lead dust. The blazing inferno in the attic had produced temperatures of up to 1900 degrees Fahrenheit, causing the scaffolding already in place for repairs to slump into a hopelessly tangled mass of scorched steel rods. But all in all, remarkably, the cathedral had lost only its spire, the roof and the timber trusses that supported it, and the central vaults. Aside from some other minor damage, the structure was basically sound, and miraculously, only a very few panels of stained glass were shattered by the falling spire.

President Macron had promised to rebuild. Now he vowed to complete the work in time for the 2024 Summer Olympics in Paris. He also suggested that perhaps the roof and spire could be rebuilt using twenty-first-century technology. Proposals poured in from all over the world, such as:

- Replicating the roof and spire, but completely in glass.
- Replicating the roof and spire, but with stained glass, lit from within.
- Rebuilding the roof as a greenhouse-covered park, with plants and animals.
- Rebuilding the spire as a gigantic prism, funneling daylight into the interior.
- Turning the entire roof into an open-air swimming pool!

Le Stryge sculpture from the gallery of chimeras

Some of these ideas are interesting; most are obviously fanciful. Official plans for the reconstruction were made while the cathedral was being cleared of all debris from the fire and toxic lead was removed from every surface.

The cleanup was a massive operation with several different tasks being performed at the same time. First, the intact vaults were covered by a temporary roof with enormous plastic tarps to keep out the weather. Netting was installed inside the cathedral to catch any falling debris. At this stage, everyone working on the site had to strip naked and shower before entering or leaving the work zone and were required to wear hazmat suits and respirators because of the hazardous lead dust coating everything. On the cathedral floor, great piles of broken stone and charred wood four feet deep were gradually cleared by remote-controlled robots. Every piece of debris was sorted, tagged, and warehoused as legally protected historical material.

Without the roof trusses helping to hold everything together, the upper walls were surprisingly vulnerable to the force of wind gusts. Enormous wooden braces weighing many tons were precision-made to fit exactly underneath each flying buttress to stiffen the structure. Debris that had landed on top of the vaults was cleared by specially trained rope technicians who rappelled down from a temporary platform. It was their job to tackle a critical part of the cleanup—the immense task of dismantling bit by bit the tangled mass of sagging steel rods from the old scaffolding that had warped and slumped from the intense heat of the fire. It all had to be done with painstaking care, so that nothing would give way and fall, further damaging the vaults.

The interior was filled with scaffolding, all surfaces were vacuumed, and a special latex coating applied and carefully peeled away to remove all traces of lead. Although undamaged by the fire, much of the stained glass was removed for cleaning and to prevent accidental damage during the rebuilding. One of the glories of Notre-Dame is its famed pipe organ. Originally built in 1730, rebuilt and enlarged in the 1860s, and upgraded with a computerized mechanical system in the 1990s, the magnificent instrument is the largest in France, with five keyboards and eight thousand pipes. It was silenced in the aftermath of the fire by the lead dust, which clogged the works and settled in the pipes. To restore it, specialists had to dismantle the delicate mechanism and clean every pipe individually.

The cleanup operation was interrupted in the spring of 2020 when the construction site was shut down for two months due to the Covid-19 pandemic. Altogether, the entire cleaning process took more than two full years, and by summer 2021 the cathedral was ready for rebuilding to begin. In

Workers rappelling down the central vaults of the crossing, which collapsed when the spire toppled

the meantime, the official decision had been made about how to proceed. All the proposals for modernizing the cathedral were rejected. The lost and damaged parts of the Cathedral of Notre-Dame would be rebuilt as it was in its "last known state," which was Viollet-le-Duc's version of the ideal Gothic cathedral. And it would be rebuilt, as much as possible, using the same materials and methods of the medieval and nineteenth-century architects, but with modern fire-prevention technology like misting systems, thermal cameras, and fire-resistant doors, as well as a recovery system to treat rainwater running off the lead roof before it goes into Paris's sewers.

When President Macron promised a speedy reconstruction, very few thought it possible. A project this complex would normally take many years, if not decades, to complete. Macron appointed General Jean-Louis Georgelin of the French army to oversee the job, and under his direction the reconstruction was planned like a military campaign with a logical order of priorities. General Georgelin was an optimistic powerhouse who was able to bypass the notoriously sluggish French bureaucracy with President Macron's support to get things done.

A great effort was made to find approximately one thousand oak trees with the right specifications from old-growth forests all over France. Each tree would provide one timber for the roof trusses, with the largest and oldest, planted before the French Revolution, reserved for the spire. The trees were rough-trimmed in a sawmill, but then each timber was shaped and finished by hand. Enormous new trusses and the internal timber structure of the new spire were first assembled off-site using the same tools and traditional methods of joinery as the medieval carpenters for absolute authenticity.

It is estimated that approximately 80 percent of the fallen stones were recovered from the debris. Those that were structurally sound could be reused. They were scanned and cataloged as 3D images, and their probable positions in the arches and vaults could be determined. Using these as templates, new stones were carved to the original specifications to fill in the blanks. Reassembling the fallen stones was like an immense 3D jigsaw puzzle. To reinforce the vaults during the rebuild, temporary wooden forms were custom crafted to fit underneath. All these materials were prepared in advance and stored away until they were needed at the right time, in the right order, for the reconstruction.

During 2023 it all began to come together. The damaged vaults were repaired, and stonemasons closed the gaping hole in the center of the **crossing** with both the intact original stones and the newly carved ones, supported by the wooden forms

Rebuilding the vaults

underneath until the mortar dried, just as the medieval stonemasons had done.

Tragically, in August 2023 General Georgelin was killed in a freak accident while trekking in the Pyrenees mountains. It is sad that he did not live to see his work completed, but by then the plans and the momentum his direction had provided were in place, and his death did little to delay the reconstruction.

In the center of the roof, a new scaffold was erected to provide a platform for the work of reassembling the timbers that had already been prepared for the new spire.

Viollet-le-Duc's magnificent spire of oak timbers and lead was re-created while hidden by the scaffold. The spire was finished by mid-December 2023, and the assembled roof trusses were lifted by enormous cranes one by one and installed over the vaults to make a new "Forest." The last major task that remained during 2024 was the installation of new lead panels over the roof, followed by months of reinstalling stained glass, removing the wooden braces from underneath the vaults and flying buttresses, cleaning the exterior, dismantling scaffolding, and finishing every detail.

President Macron's deadline for completion by the 2024 Paris Olympics was missed, but only by a few months, thanks to the tireless efforts and expertise of hundreds of workers and craftspeople who dedicated their talents to the reconstruction of the Cathedral of Notre-Dame as a kind of crusade. As one of the carpenters remarked, "Did you ever think you'd be able to look at Notre-Dame and say, 'I built that'?"

Viollet-le-Duc's spire had been topped by a large copper weather vane in the form of a rooster, a traditional emblem of France. When the spire collapsed during the fire, it was presumed that the weather vane was destroyed. But it had merely become detached and was found in the debris the next day, battered but intact. During the days of despair following the catastrophe, recovering the old weather vane was regarded as a much-needed symbol of hope. A new rooster weather vane was designed for the new spire, this time made of copper covered with gold. It has wings shaped like flames, recalling the phoenix, the mythical bird that lives for five hundred years and then expires in a blaze of glory, only to be reborn fully grown from the ashes, over and over for all eternity.

The new rooster weather vane topping off the reconstructed spire

EPILOGUE

THE WORLD'S CATHEDRAL

On December 7, 2024, the eagerly awaited official reopening of Notre-Dame began with the ringing of the cathedral bells. The archbishop of Paris knocked on the main portal with a staff of timber from the old Forest that had survived the fire, and the doors were opened for a televised event attended by dignitaries and donors from around the world. French President Emmanuel Macron gave an address thanking the firefighters and the experts, technicians, and artisans who worked on the cathedral, and a message from Pope Francis was read. There followed a short religious service with music from the restored organ and cathedral choir, and a procession of banners. The inaugural Mass was celebrated the next morning, December 8, with a congregation of dignitaries, and later that day there was yet another Mass, which was open to the public. Eight days of special services rounded out the grand reopening.

The newly cleaned interior of Notre-Dame is a stunning revelation. Stripped of the grime of centuries, the clean, bare limestone gleams surprisingly pale and white. It is resplendent. The rebuilt and refreshed old church has a new lease on life. But weather and urban pollution attack the exterior limestone relentlessly. The porous rock absorbs water that combines with pollutants in the air to make acid, and the surface of the stone gradually crumbles away bit by bit. In old photographs the fifty-four beasts in the gallery of chimeras have sharp edges and crisp details. But after 150 years they are worn down and eroded. Some were hardly more than irregular stumps. A few were so ruined that they have been replaced with modern copies.

The catastrophe of April 15, 2019, and the campaign of reconstruction riveted the attention of people from all over the world. By almost losing it forever, we gained a new appreciation of Notre-Dame's importance as the ultimate example of a Gothic cathedral. As a monument of three different eras—the Middle Ages, the nineteenth century, and now the twenty-first century—the newly refurbished cathedral has reclaimed its official place as the Cathedral of Paris, a symbol of France, a great milestone in the cultural heritage of humanity, and one of the most popular tourist attractions on Earth. And unofficially, more than ever before, the Cathedral of Notre-Dame may be celebrated as the World's Cathedral.

NOTE FROM THE EDITOR

Lynn Curlee and I began working together in 2024. He had previously published several books, an impressive collection of beautifully illustrated nonfiction picture books that included the Robert F. Sibert Honor Book *Brooklyn Bridge,* among other acclaimed titles, with Atheneum Books for Young Readers. As soon as we began working together on *Notre-Dame,* I was immediately struck by Lynn's passion for his craft and his enthusiasm to be working on a topic he was so excited about: the majestic cathedral of Notre-Dame and how it had almost been completely destroyed by fire in 2019. I found him to be thoughtful, methodical, and hardworking, and, most notably, there was within him a joy for life and for art that came through in every interaction we had.

During the production process, Lynn painstakingly painted by hand all the illustrations in this book using traditional media. He would send me and our art director a photo of the works in progress to keep us updated. Each painting was then photographed professionally to ensure high resolution.

But one day, when nearly all the art was already completed, emails from Lynn stopped coming. In early 2025 Lynn became ill and was unable to continue working. With Lynn's support and help from both his agent and partner, Nicholas Atkins, our production team continued moving forward and finished *Notre-Dame* in his honor. While this book is likely Lynn's last book with us, his legacy of gorgeously crafted nonfiction books, his appreciation for beauty and art, and his exuberance and passion for life itself will never be forgotten.

Kristie Choi, Editor for Atheneum Books for Young Readers

NOTRE-DAME STATISTICS

Length: 420 feet
Width: 157 feet
Nave dimensions: 196 × 42 feet
Choir dimensions: 124 × 39 feet
Transept dimensions: 157 × 46 feet
Height of vaults: 108 feet
Height including the roof: 141 feet
Height of towers: 226 feet
Height of spire: 315 feet
Span of largest flying buttress: 49 feet
Western façade rose window diameter: 31.8 feet
Transept rose windows diameter: 43 feet
Number of windows: 113
Bells: Notre-Dame has 10 bronze bells in its main bell towers. The oldest and largest was cast in 1686, weighs 14.3 tons, and is named Emmanuel.

INTERESTING FACTS

- During the firefight on April 15, 2019, with the roof ablaze high above them, cathedral authorities scrambled to remove and secure valuable precious objects and irreplaceable holy relics. They made a human chain to efficiently get as much out as they could.

- In the Middle Ages, architects are rarely mentioned and are known instead as "master" builders. The name of Notre-Dame's first architect is unknown. In the cathedral's second building phase, from the mid-thirteenth to mid-fourteenth centuries, the master builders are identified as Jean de Chelles, Pierre de Montreuil, and Pierre de Chelles.

- Nearly 250 companies and art workshops from all over France and a total of more than 2,000 people were involved in the cleanup and reconstruction of Notre-Dame. Their names are listed in a document preserved in a sealed tube inside the new golden rooster weather vane. The entire cleanup and rebuilding campaign is estimated to have cost approximately $765,000,000. More than 340,000 donors from 150 countries all around the world contributed more than $928,000,000 to the effort.

- Pérotin was a composer who created music at Notre-Dame in the years around 1200. You can hear this hauntingly beautiful, ethereal music today by searching for Pérotin on YouTube, and be magically transported in your imagination back to the Middle Ages.

- For a wonderful, comprehensive account of exactly how the Gothic cathedrals were built, take a look at *Cathedral: The Story of Its Construction* by David Macaulay. He takes you step by step through the entire construction process with spectacular, detailed, and evocative illustrations. It's a classic.

GLOSSARY

Aisle—the spaces parallel to the nave and choir on each side, with lower vaults above them.

Apse—the semicircular space at the eastern end of the choir, with the altar.

Balustrade—a row of small columns topped by a rail.

Basilica—a church plan with a lofty central nave and choir, lower side aisles, and often including an apse.

Belfry—the wooden framework that supports the church bells, inside a tower.

Buttress—a solid pier, often made of stone or wood, that strengthens a wall.

Cathedral—the home church of a bishop.

Chimera—a fanciful carved creature that seems to guard the cathedral.

Choir—the eastern central space of the church, which is reserved for the clergy and choral singers.

Clerestory—the upper walls of the nave and choir with large windows.

Crocket—a small, sharply projecting decorative element common in Gothic architecture.

Crossing—the intersection of the nave/choir and the transept at the center of the church.

Finial—a decorative element that is typically pointed and placed at the top of a structure or spire.

Flying buttress—a stone arch that transfers the weight of a vault to an external pier.

Gargoyle—a stone rainspout usually in the form of a monstrous creature.

Nave—the western central space of the church, where the laypeople congregate.

Pier—a solid stone pillar that supports an arch.

Portal—an opening in a wall that is often a grand doorway or entrance for an important structure or building.

Rib—a stone arch that reinforces and carries the weight of a vault.

Rose window—a very large circular stained-glass window, divided into segments.

Transept—the area of the church that separates the nave from the choir at right angles, giving the church the form of a cross.

Trusses—triangular wooden frames that support the roof.

Turret—a small vertical tower that sticks out from the wall of a building, sometimes from the corner.

Vault—a self-supporting arched structure of stone. A series of vaults form the ceiling of the church.

BIBLIOGRAPHY

Borrus, Kathy. *Notre Dame de Paris*. Black Dog & Leventhal, 2019.

Camille, Michael. *The Gargoyles of Notre-Dame*. University of Chicago Press, 2009.

Felix, Antonia. *Notre-Dame de Paris*. Sterling, 2019.

Kunzig, Robert. "Notre Dame After the Fire." *National Geographic*, February 2022.

Macaulay, David. *Cathedral*. Houghton Mifflin Harcourt, 1973. Revised edition with new color illustrations, 2013.

Peltier, Elian, et al. "Notre-Dame Came Far Closer to Collapsing than People Knew. This Is How It Was Saved." *New York Times*, July 18, 2019. https://www.nytimes.com/interactive/2019/07/16/world/europe/notre-dame.html.

Sandron, Dany, and Andrew Tallon. *Notre Dame Cathedral*. Penn State University Press, 2013.

Simmons, Keir, et al. "The Comeback of Notre Dame: American Builders Help to Restore Iconic Paris Landmark." NBC News, April 15, 2024. https://www.nbcnews.com/news/world/france-paris-notre-dame-cathedral-fire-restoration-macron-carpenter-rcna147621.

Swaan, Wim. *The Gothic Cathedral*. Doubleday, 1969.

Zachmann, Patrick. *Restoring Notre-Dame de Paris*. Schiffer, 2024.

— For Nick —

ATHENEUM BOOKS FOR YOUNG READERS
An imprint of Simon & Schuster Children's Publishing Division
1230 Avenue of the Americas, New York, New York 10020

For information about special discounts for bulk purchases, please contact Simon & Schuster Special Sales at 1-866-506-1949 or business@simonandschuster.com.

Simon & Schuster strongly believes in freedom of expression and stands against censorship in all its forms. For more information, visit BooksBelong.com.

The Simon & Schuster Speakers Bureau can bring authors to your live event. For more information or to book an event, contact the Simon & Schuster Speakers Bureau at 1-866-248-3049 or visit our website at www.simonspeakers.com.

The text for this book was set in Deepdene URW.

The illustrations for this book were rendered in acrylic on canvas.

Mr. Curlee would like to thank Josh Gaddy for photographing the paintings.

Manufactured in China

1225 SCP

First Edition

10 9 8 7 6 5 4 3 2 1

Library of Congress Cataloging-in-Publication Data
Names: Curlee, Lynn, 1947- author illustrator
Title: Notre-Dame : the world's cathedral / Lynn Curlee.
Description: First edition. | New York : Atheneum Books for Young Readers, [2025] | Includes bibliographical references. |
Summary: "On April 15, 2019, the Cathedral of Notre-Dame in Paris was almost destroyed by fire, an event that shocked and riveted the entire world as it played out in real time on TV and across the internet. In *Notre-Dame*, award-winning author-illustrator Lynn Curlee builds a thrilling narrative around the story of the fire and its aftermath, along with the rebuilding of the historic cathedral, including captivating information about cathedrals, gothic architecture, French history (even Quasimodo, the famous hunchback of Notre-Dame!), restoration of old buildings, heroism under fire, and the renovation of the World's Cathedral."—Provided by publisher.
Identifiers: LCCN 2025013724 | ISBN 9781665971836 (hardcover) | ISBN 9781665971850 (ebook)
Subjects: LCSH: Notre-Dame de Paris (Cathedral)—Fire, 2019—Juvenile literature | Catholic church buildings—Reconstruction—France—Paris—History—21st century—Juvenile literature | LCGFT: Literature.
Classification: LCC NA5550.N7 C87 2025 | DDC 726.6/40944361—dc23/eng/20250519
LC record available at https://lccn.loc.gov/2025013724